From Cuba to United States

by Maritza Lopez Garcia

NATIONAL GEOGRAPHIC LEARNING | CENGAGE

T0061137

It is 90 miles from Florida to Cuba.

My name is Maritza. I am from Matanzas. It is a city in Cuba.

Now I live in Miami, Florida.

This is my family.

My mother—Maria
Garcia de Lopez

My father—Ramon Lopez

Papi and Mateo

My brothers—Mateo Lopez Garcia; Luis Lopez Garcia

Luis is such a clown!

My aunt and uncle live in Miami.

Aunt Isabel   Uncle Jorge

Their dog, Dante

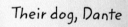

They met us at the airport.

TARJETA DE EMBARQUE (Boarding Pass)

NOMBRE / NAME

DE / FROM NASSAU
A / TO MIAMI

VUELO / FLIGHT   CLASE-CLASS   FECHA / DATE SALIDA / TIME
PC 7830 Y   31JAN20:30

PUERTA / GATE EMBARQUE / BOARDING ASIENTO / SEAT
56   14:10   4E   NO

EQUIPAJE / BAGGAGE   005

MIAMI INTERNATIONAL AIRPORT

I miss my home in Cuba.

My home in Matanzas

¡Saludos de Matanzas!

The beach in Matanzas

But my new home in Miami is nice!

MY NEW ROOM!

The color of
my room

I have a lot of friends in Matanzas.

My friends in Cuba

Elena and Alicia

HECTOR!

¡Hola, Maritza!

¿Cómo te va? ¿Te gusta vivir
en Miami? ¿Tienes muchos
nuevos amigos?

Alicia y yo te extrañamos y
pensamos mucho en ti.
Aquí te envío una foto de
nosotras dos.

Escríbenos pronto.

Elena

Elena

Now I have many friends in Miami!

My friends, Dalili and Andrea

My friends and I go to the movies.

Friendship

We go to parties.

Happy Birthday

For : Carlos

Date : Saturday   Time : 5:00

Place : Andrea's House

R. S. V. P. 555-1234

Miami is a lot like Cuba.

Little Havana is a Cuban neighborhood in Miami.

People dance to salsa music at a street party.

I can find Cuban food here!

I LOVE good Cuban food.

The flag of Cuba

I miss Matanzas. But I like Miami, too!

16